DISCOVERING SHAPES

TRIANGLES

SANDY RIGGS

■

ART BY RICHARD MACCABE

BENCHMARK BOOKS

MARSHALL CAVENDISH
NEW YORK

Benchmark Books
Marshall Cavendish Corporation
99 White Plains Road
Tarrytown, New York 10591-9001

©Marshall Cavendish Corporation, 1997

Series created by Blackbirch Graphics, Inc.

Printed and bound in the United States.

Library of Congress Cataloging-in-Publication Data

Riggs, Sandy
    Triangles / by Sandy Riggs: art by Richard Maccabe.
        p.   cm. — (Discovering shapes)
    Includes index.
    Summary: Identifies various triangles found in familiar objects and uses activities, puzzles, and games to explore this shape.
    ISBN 0-7614-0459-7 (lib. bdg.)
    1. Triangle—Juvenile literature. [1. Triangle. 2. Shape. 3. Amusement.] I. Maccabe, Richard, ill. II. Title. III. Series.
QA482.R54   1997
793.7'4—dc20

                                                 96-3173
                                                  CIP
                                                    AC

Contents

■ ■ ■ ■ ■ ■ ■

Keeping Warm Under Triangles

Quilts have been around for thousands of years, keeping people warm. But in colonial America, quilts became something special. Imaginative quilt makers created quilt designs—patterns that were colorful, fun, and full of shapes.

Here's an early quilt design called Ships at Sea. Find the square that is repeated throughout the quilt. How many triangles are used in one square?

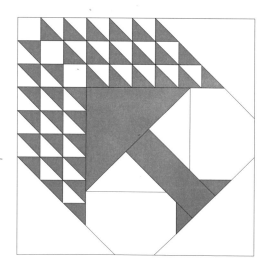

This pattern is called Pine Tree. How many triangles are in this one square alone? How many triangles do you think a whole quilt would have? Do you think that "thousands" might be a good guess?

Early quilt makers invented some patterns by folding paper. They would start with a square, fold it several times, and end up with a number of triangles.

Look at this design called Whirligig. Can you see a square folded into triangles in Whirligig's design? How many sizes of triangles are there? What colors are they? What is a whirligig anyway?

What do you see in this quilt pattern? First trace the pattern. Then color the triangles to show the design. The name is a clue. The colors are up to you.

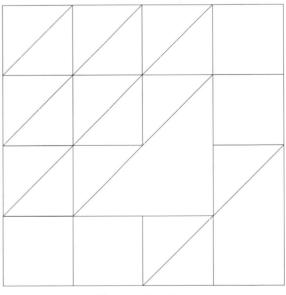

Flower Basket

The Great Triangle Spying Contest

Set up this contest with some friends. Here's the challenge: See who can make the longest list of things that are shaped like a triangle. You may work alone, with partners, or in teams.

When you spy a triangle, write down the name of the object. Then write the part of it that is a triangle. You can even add a neat sketch. Your list might look like this:

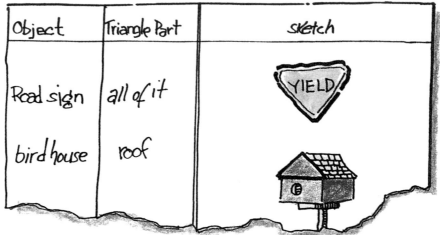

Object	Triangle Part	Sketch
Road sign	all of it	YIELD
bird house	roof	

Did you notice any roofs when you were out and about looking for triangles? Which kind of roof do you think is the most common? Dome-shaped? Flat? Triangle-shaped?

Find as many photos of city skylines as you can in books and magazines. Record the numbers of the different kinds of roofs.

Which kind of roof scored the highest in your survey? Are you surprised?

"Tri" These Toothpick Puzzles

Solve the puzzles about toothpicks. Think about triangles and draw the "picks." Or you might use real toothpicks.

• George Grin took some toothpicks, stuck the points in clay, and made a triangle. There are eleven toothpicks standing on each side of his triangle. How many toothpicks did George use altogether to make the triangle?

• Can you move three of the toothpicks to make a triangle that points up instead of down? Give it a "tri."

Want a hint for the last puzzle? Use 3-D thinking.

• Make four triangles with nine toothpicks. Nothing to it, you might say. Then make four with only six toothpicks by looking at it a new way.

Origami

Origami is a clever way of folding paper and shapes. Fold the triangles shown in the steps below, and you'll end up with an origami penguin.

1. Trace and cut out this triangle. Fold it along the dotted line. Use paper with a color on one side or color a plain piece of paper on one side.

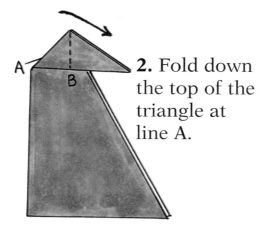

2. Fold down the top of the triangle at line A.

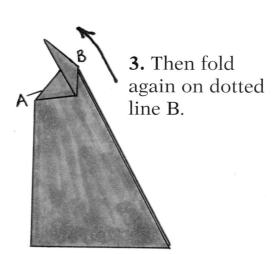

3. Then fold again on dotted line B.

4. Pull the top of the triangle up. Open the triangle slightly and push the top down. The fold should be at line A to make the penguin's neck.

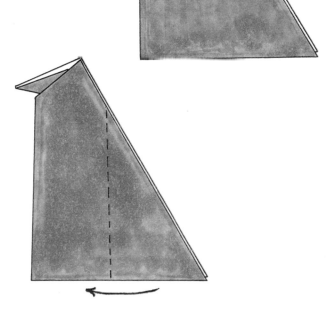

5. Again, open the triangle slightly and pull the tip of the triangle up and push into the neck at line B. This will make the penguin's bill.

6. Now fold the sides of the big triangle forward to make the wings of the penguin.

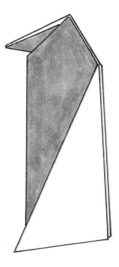

Beautiful Barns

In Pennsylvania, there are barns decorated with big, beautiful star signs. Early settlers who came to Pennsylvania from Germany painted the first signs—always a star inside a circle. Because the star had six points, the signs were called hex signs. *Hex* came from *sechs*, the German word for "six."

Farmers invented hundreds of different designs. They liked to use bright, cheerful colors.

Look carefully at the 6-pointed star in this simple design. Can you find the two triangles that form it? Try drawing the triangles to make the star.

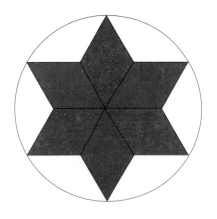

How were triangles used in the design of this star? Mark the center of your sketch and try drawing the design. Color it with two colors you like.

Over the years, many star makers let their imaginations soar. They created star signs with 8 points, 12 points, and even 16 points!

Let *your* imagination soar. Use a ruler to make a triangle with equal sides. You may trace this one if you would like. Make a circle that the triangle will fit inside. You can trace around something like a jar lid or a can to draw a circle. Use the triangle and the circle to design a hex sign. You can make as many points as you want to!

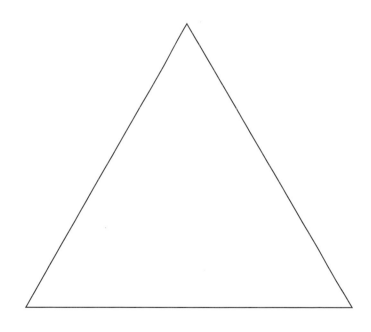

Can you figure out a way to draw a 6-pointed star inside a 6-pointed star?

Tangram Triangles

This Chinese puzzle is thousands of years old. It is called a tangram. Trace this square on a sheet of construction paper. Then cut out the seven puzzle pieces.

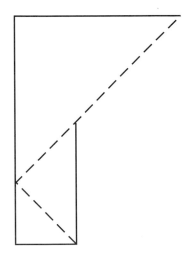

Take a look at your tangram pieces. How many pieces are triangles? How are the triangles alike? How are they different? How are they related to each other?

See what figures you can form, using any three or four of the triangles. Here's an example of a 5-sided figure. Can you make another 5-sided figure? A 6-sided figure? A 7-sided figure? How about an 8-sided figure?

Examine these congruent triangles very carefully. Check them
out with a friend. Decide whether the second one in each pair
was **flipped** over, **slid** to the side, or **turned** up or down. By
the way, do this in your heads.

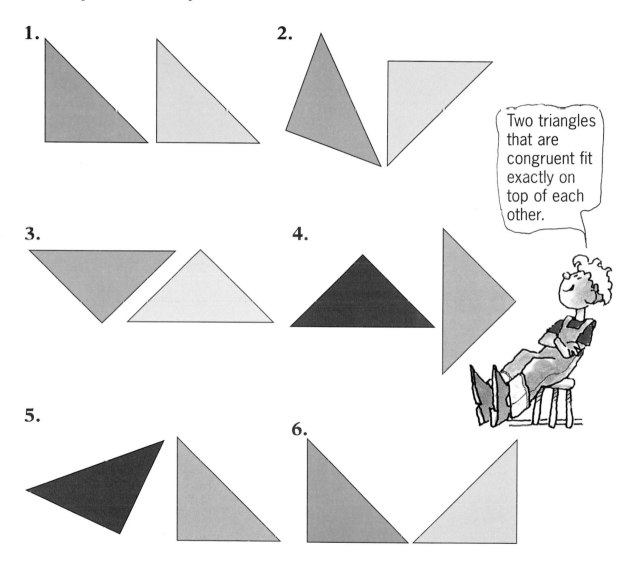

Two triangles
that are
congruent fit
exactly on
top of each
other.

Now use your tangram triangles to "check your
heads." Fit one triangle on another by flipping,
sliding, or turning it.

13

Congruent Concentration

Find a friend or two and play this matching card game. First, get set up and read the rules. Then get ready to concentrate.

You will need to:

• Get a sheet of construction paper, scissors, a ruler, and a pencil.

• Measure the size of one card on the next page.

• Cut twelve pieces of construction paper about the same size as the card.

• Get ten markers, such as pennies, paper clips, or buttons.

How to play:

Two triangles are congruent to each other if they have the same shape and size.

• Cover each card on page 15 with a slip of paper.

• Play the game like concentration. Take turns uncovering two cards at a time.

• If the triangles are congruent, keep the slips.

Then place a marker on each card to show that these cards are out of play. Take another turn.

• If the triangles are not congruent, put the slips back where they were. The other player then takes a turn.

• Play until all cards are uncovered. The player with the most slips of paper is the winner and the best concentrator—at least for this round.

The Mighty Triangle

Shapes hold things together, including awesome things like buildings and bridges. Long ago, builders discovered the importance of the triangle. A framework of triangles is the strongest design of all. Find out for yourself. You'll need these "building supplies":

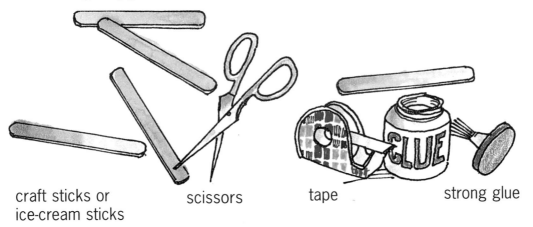

craft sticks or
ice-cream sticks

scissors

tape

strong glue

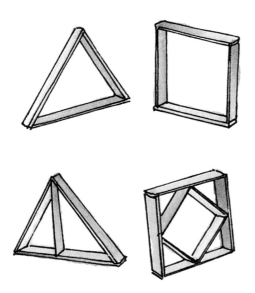

• Make a square by taping four sticks together. Then press on the sides of the square. What happens? Now take three sticks and make a triangle. What happens when you press on the sides of the triangle?

• You can make the square stronger by adding triangles to its corners. And you can even make the triangle stronger by adding a "post" and making two triangles. Try it. Cut some sticks and glue them like these.

Smart bridge builders put beams together to form a chain of triangles. This framework is called a triangular truss. Here is one design for a truss bridge.

• Draw or construct (with your sticks) some other triangular truss designs. Which of your designs is the strongest? Why?

Now try this with a friend. Build a geodesic dome by connecting triangles. Have you ever heard of this kind of building? It seems like it's all roof because it's all dome.

• Get some clay and straws. Roll clay balls, snip straws (about 4 inches long), and start putting triangles together. Can you make a dome shape? Is it strong? Why?

Running Around the Labyrinth

The creature in the corner is a Minotaur. The Minotaur—part bull and part man—is a character from a Greek myth. A king put the Minotaur in this maze of passages. It's called a labyrinth. The Minotaur never got out of the labyrinth. Play this game with a friend and see if you can.

You will need:

twelve slips of paper
numbered 1 through 12

a calculator

paper and pencil
for keeping score

The perimeter of a triangle is the distance around its three sides. You need to add the lengths of the sides.

How to play:

1. Put the numbered slips face down and take turns picking one.

2. Find the part of the labyrinth that has the number you get.

3. Figure out the perimeter of that triangle.

4. Write down the number as your score.

5. Keep running around the labyrinth and adding perimeters together.

6. The first player to get a total score of 200 or higher wins—and ESCAPES!

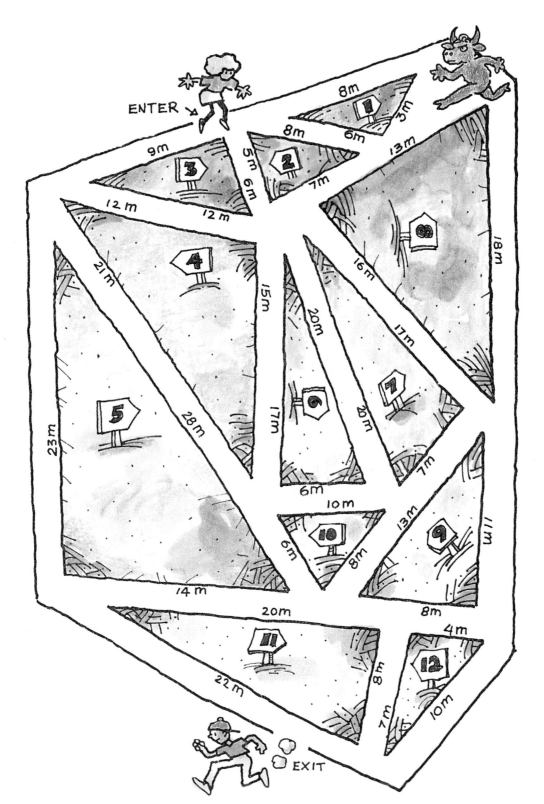

ENTER

EXIT

Fold and Find

Trace and cut out this triangle. Then figure out how to fold it so you end up with sixteen small triangles. The first fold and one small triangle are shown. All sixteen triangles should be this size. You must fold only. No drawing allowed!

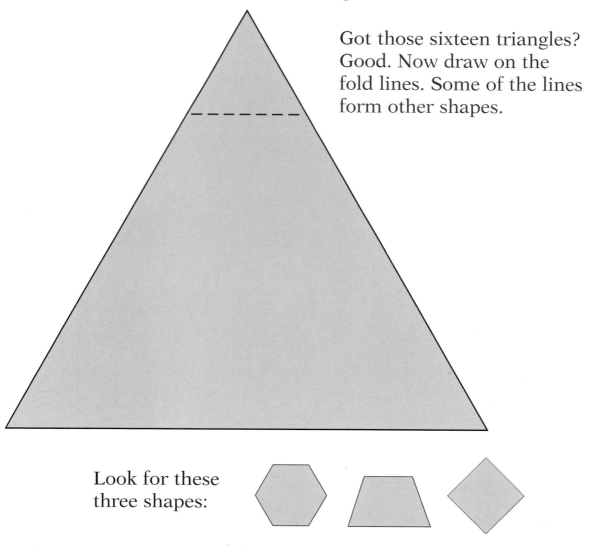

Got those sixteen triangles? Good. Now draw on the fold lines. Some of the lines form other shapes.

Look for these three shapes:

Can you name some of them? See if you can cut out all three shapes, but be sure before you snip. No taping allowed! How many triangles form each shape? How many triangles are left?

Eye Teasers

How many triangles can you find in this *Tyrannosaurus rex*? When full grown, *T. rex* weighed about eight tons. Did you know that scientists think dinosaurs might have had colorful skin with wild patterns?

A quadrilateral has four sides.

Find how many triangles and quadrilaterals are in each figure. A triangle is worth five points. A quadrilateral is worth six points. Figure out which figure is worth more. How close are the values of the two figures?

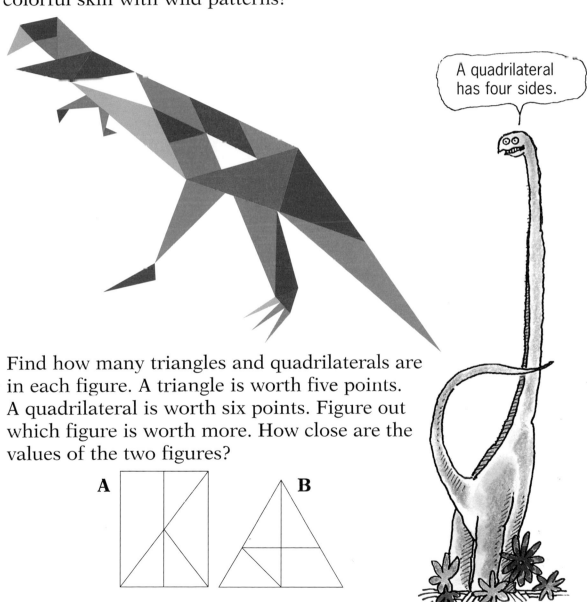

A

B

Tic-Tac-Toe Angles

Here's a tic-tac-toe game. Challenge a friend to play with you. You'll need five markers each. One player could use pennies, and the other could use nickels.

How to play:

• Take turns choosing a space. Name the kind of angle in the space: right, acute, or obtuse. If you're correct, put a marker in the space.

• The first player to make a row of three markers wins. The row can go across, up and down, or from corner to corner.

• If no player makes a row of three, the game is a tie.

A right angle is the shape of a square corner.

An equilateral triangle has three sides the same length.

An isosceles triangle has at least two sides the same length.

A scalene triangle has no sides the same length.

Riding the Streaker

Climb aboard the Streaker Roller Coaster—if you dare—and play this fun game with a couple of friends.

You will need:

• a different marker for each player (You could use a paper clip, a penny, and a pebble.)

• paper for drawing

• a pencil

• a number cube or one die from a pair of dice

How to play:

1. Put your markers on GOING UP.

2. Take turns throwing the die. If you throw a 1, 2, 3, or 4, move that number of spaces. If you throw a 5 or 6, take another turn.

3. When you land on a TRIANGLE space, you must draw an example of the triangle named. If your fellow riders agree it's correct, move ahead one more space.

4. If you land on a DIZZY space, a SCREAM space, or a LOOP space, do what it says.

5. Of course, the first rider to STREAK DOWN wins.

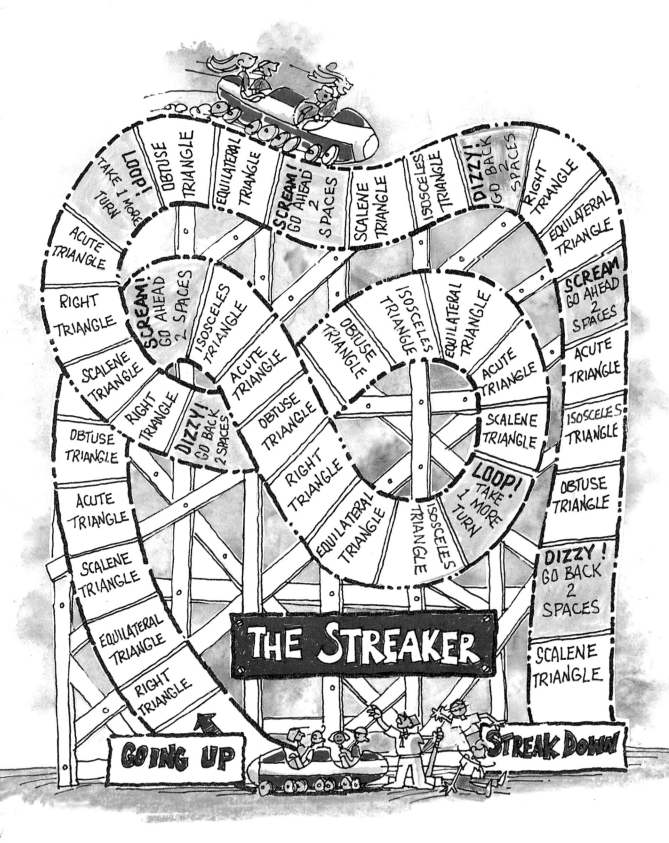

Eye Challengers

Answer the questions about the dots—lots of dots. First find the small triangle, the middle-sized triangle, and the large triangle.

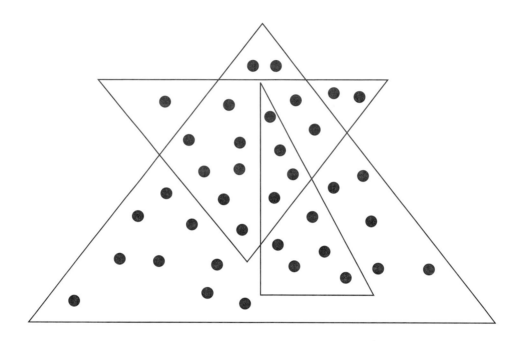

1. How many dots are in the middle-sized triangle but not in the other two triangles?

2. How many dots are in the small triangle but not in the other two triangles?

3. How many dots are in the middle-sized triangle that are also in the large triangle but not in the small triangle?

4. How many dots are in the large triangle that are also in the middle-sized triangle and also in the small triangle?

Answers

Pps. 4–5, Keeping Warm Under Triangles

Ships at Sea: There are 10 triangles in one square.

Pine Tree: There are 74 triangles in one Pine Tree square! "Thousands" would be a good guess because a quilt could have 30 squares, for example, and 30 x 74 = 2,220.

Whirligig: There are triangles of three sizes: 4 small orange triangles, 4 large orange triangles, 4 medium blue triangles, and 4 large blue triangles. A whirligig is a pinwheel.

Flower Basket:

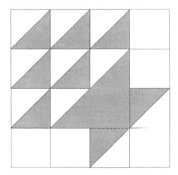

P. 6, The Great Triangle Spying Contest

Surveys will vary, but triangle-shaped roofs are common for houses. Flat roofs are common for factories and high-rise buildings.

P. 7, "Tri" These Toothpick Puzzles

George used 30 toothpicks altogether. One way to solve the puzzle is to add the toothpicks on the three sides (33). Each toothpick at a corner, however, is on two sides of the triangle. This means you have included each of these toothpicks two times in your sum, so you have to subtract the 3 extra ones to get the answer: 33 – 3 = 30.

By moving the end toothpicks from the top row and the toothpick from the bottom row to the positions shown, you can make the triangle point up.

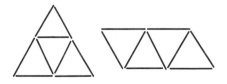

Here are two ways you can make four triangles with nine toothpicks.

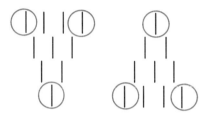

You can make four triangles with six toothpicks by forming a triangular pyramid, which has four faces that are triangles.

Pps. 8-9, Origami

No answers.

Pps. 10-11, Beautiful Barns

Here are the two triangles that form the star.

Here is a 6-pointed star inside a 6-pointed star.

Pps. 12–13, Tangram Triangles

Here are possible figures:

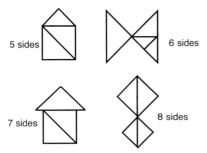

1. slid 2. turned 3. flipped 4. turned
5. turned 6. flipped

Pps. 14–15, Congruent Concentration

There are six pairs of congruent triangles.

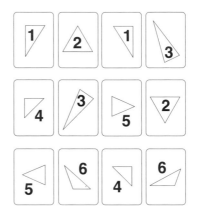

Pps. 16–17, The Mighty Triangle

Here are possible triangular truss designs:

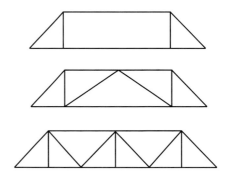

Pps. 18–19, Running Around the Labyrinth

No answers.

P. 20, Fold and Find

The shapes are a hexagon (6 triangles), a trapezoid (3 triangles) ,and a rhombus (2 triangles). There are 5 triangles left.

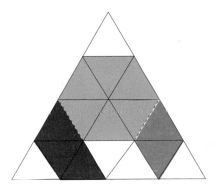

P. 21, Eye Teasers

There are 40 triangles in *T. rex*: 13 in the head, 12 in the legs, and 15 in the body and tail. Figure A is worth 71 points (7 triangles, 6 quadrilaterals), and Figure B, 69 points (9 triangles, 4 quadrilaterals).

Pps. 22–23, Tic-Tac-Toe Angles

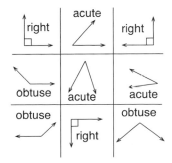

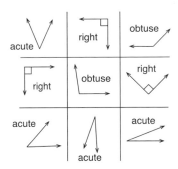

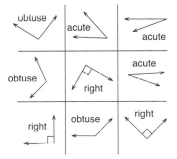

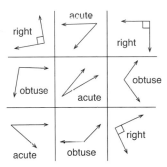

Pps. 24–25, Riding the Streaker

No answers.

P. 26, Eye Challengers

1. 3 dots **2.** 0 dots **3.** 9 dots **4.** 4 dots.

Glossary

acute angle An angle that is less than a right angle.

example

acute triangle A triangle that has three acute angles.

congruent triangles Triangles that have the same size and shape.

dome A large, rounded roof.

equilateral triangle A triangle that has three sides the same length.

flipped Picked up and turned over.

geodesic dome A dome-shaped building made by connecting panels that are the same shape, often triangles.

isosceles triangle A triangle that has at least two sides the same length.

obtuse angle An angle that is greater than a right angle.

example

obtuse triangle A triangle that has one obtuse angle.

perimeter The distance around a shape.

quadrilateral A shape that has four sides.

right angle An angle that has the shape of a square corner.

example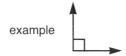

right triangle A triangle that has one right angle.

scalene triangle A triangle that has no sides the same length.

slid Moved without picking up.

square A shape that has four sides the same length.

triangle A shape that has three sides.

triangular truss A framework of beams that form triangles.

turned Moved around a point in a circular direction.

Index